YOUNG
YOUNG QUEEN

by: Justin Sims

Illustrations by:

Jasmine Mills

Dedication

This book is a special handwritten letter written to encourage, engage, motivate and move young girls and women of color to simply live their best life and always be the best version of themselves that they can be.

Please read, reread, take notes, write in, highlight, share, and discuss with your family and friends.

This book is yours, be open and allow it to inspire the greatness within you.

This is for you, young Queen.

DEDICATION

I would like to give a salute and a "i see you" to all of the current Queen's making it happen today. (By far these aren't the only women making impact, this is just some that I wanted to give a shoutout to and these are also name's that Young Queen's can research in their spare time for motivation) Michelle Obama, Auntie Waters, Oprah, Beyonce, Cree Summers, Ava Duvernay, Issa Rae, Lena Waithe, Jada Pinkett and Willow Smith, Karen Civil, Susan Taylor, Marsai Martin, Beverly Bond, Lauren Simmons, Mo'ne Davis, Stephanie Lampkin, Tiffany Budgetnista Aliche, Miss USA Cheslie Kryst, Miss Teen USA Kaliegh Garris, and Miss America 19 Nia Franklin, Gina Toellese, Tarana Burke, Jesica Disu, Jemele Hill, Arlan Hamilton, Brittany K Barnett, MiAngel Cody, Keisha Lance Bottoms, Stacey Abrams, Jewel Burkes Solomon, Jamira Burley, Symone Sanders, Victoria Sanders, Jordan Howard, Dr Hadiya Green, Melissa Kimble, Courtney Whitaker, Janaya Griffin, Jasmine Edwards, Chocolate Milk Mommies, Dr. Kimberly Nettles, Jasmine Clennon, Dr. Taneidra Walker, Brea Baker, Brianna Baker, Scottie Beam, Imani Ellis, Brittany Oliver, Misty Copeland, Ibithaj Muhammad, Maya Moore, Brehanna Daniels, Kiko Davis, Zakia Bain, Slick Woods, Megan Ward, Dena Simmons, Lauren Underwood, Raynell Steward (Supa Cent), Meghan Spears, Tiffany Loftin, Alencia Johnson, Alicia Garza, Tsion Gurmu, and Opal Tometi.

Acknowledgements

My mother, Pandora Robinson Sims, and Genice Hertzfeld Great Aunt and Godmother, thanks for the continuous inspiration and unwavering kindness, RIP and Thank you

My granddaddy, Leonard Payne for being a dedicated reader

Reginald Jackson, friend/brother for writing me on Instagram and saying it was time.

Mike Gottfried, Tracy Hipps, and Dr. Cunningham for providing me with structured mentoring opportunities.

Jada Pearson, Imari Curtis, Stephen Storey, and Mario Addison for consistently checking on me during the process.

Megan Alston and Dreena Whitfield.

Khiry, Geli, Kim Dees, Jwow, Tesa, FM Supreme and C Rogers for really hearing me out, giving me real feedback, chopping the book up, and pumping me up early on!

UAB's Information Engineering Management program, thanks for pushing me to the next level.

"The Savages" – for constant pressure.

Serena Williams for being at the top of her game for so long and displaying Queenly traits for all young women to mimic.

Michelle Obama for encouraging Young Queens across the World and truly changing the narrative.

Last but not least, all purchasers, readers, and recommenders of this book, this is for you. Thank you

To: _____

From: _____

Foreword
Author Curtrice L. Williams

Social media has become the gateway to so many opportunities and connections with others. Actually, this is exactly how I began using the gifts God's gifts on a larger scale. After my start blogging and editing for a website for some time, in 2014, I began a new journey writing on Instagram with a mission to reach as many women's hearts and minds as possible. I had a vision to see more whole and genuinely happy women who can work together to ensure our children, our future leaders, know the importance of self-love and respect as well as understand positive relationship, healthy self-care practices, boundary setting, accountability and many other traits that essentially lead to healthier individuals and set the tone for our youth's brighter futures. I never imagined the lives that would be touched along this journey. Every day I hope to inspire, to encourage, uplift, and pour into others in a positive way. By walking in my purpose, I was able to connect with Justin, who has also to me humbly being a part of this beautiful book that will touch the lives of so many.

I remember two years ago Justin brought this idea to me and asked questions about writing as he took interest in my book, "This Isn't It: Reviving the Woman Within". At the time, I was a newly published author and knew the tremendous difference sharing your heart within a book could make. I know that writing is an art and through creativity, eyes can be opened, and lives can be changed. Therefore, two years later when Justin invited me to write this foreword, I felt so incredibly blessed that his idea turned to effort and came to fruition. I watched both his efforts and desire to create change within his city, and his outreach to be a vessel used to set an example for our children. His heart is so big, and it is evident in not only his words, but how he operates in his daily life. He is a walking example of what it means to have a desire and a dream, to work hard, and to make what happen. Many people say that they want to write a book one day or that they want to help create a positive change, but not everyone makes it a priority and takes the necessary steps to create in this capacity. I am so glad that Justin did. I feel his readers will know by his example that they too can follow their dreams and that if they don't give up, possibilities are endless.

The young queens who will read the pages within this book will be stronger, better and wiser. They will be encouraged and equipped to flourish through the learning moments in life because doing so has a great deal to do with confidence and confidence speaks so loudly within the pages Justin has written. Readers will be better able to maintain healthy relationships with others and will know that it's important to surround themselves with those whose light shines bright, as opposed to tolerating connections that are unhealthy. This book is so needed today in a world where so many are misguided. As social media was mentioned in a positive light during my opening, we can't ignore the fact the it has also been a source of many insecurities within our children. From cyber bullying to depictions that everyone's life is so perfect and everyone's opinions on what is beautiful and what is not, social media has also had negative effects and sometimes this has even led to fatal outcomes, but a book like this speaks life and will help our young queens see their value and understand their power no matter what they may see or experience. This book will help cultivate healthy perspectives and will play a part in affirming who they are no matter what someone else may tell them.

When I wrote my book, I remember coming up with the first part of the title, "This Isn't It" and as soon as I began reading "Young Queen, Young Queen, a part of it really resonated with me. "I know that life will get tough at times, but please, don't give up, and don't be afraid to ask for help". This is one of the many parts that made me smile as it reminds me so much of my own mantra. Our young black girls need to see a book with little girls who look like them, they need the reminder early on that no matter what happens, it's not the end; they are still beautiful, strong, needed, and absolutely not alone. Before my book was released, I prayed that every reader would be blessed by it and I pray the very same regarding "Young Queen, Young Queen." Every mother and father with a young queen will be blessed by adding this to the family library. This is a great way to initiate spending more family time and making sure we equip our children for life when we are not around. What we teach them will follow them no matter what they do and where they go in life. As a mother, this book excites me. So, thank you Justin for your timely and touching contribution to the literary world.

Young Queen, Young Queen

You are awesome, amazing, and beautifully hand-crafted.

Young Queen, Young Queen

You can do, and you can be
anything you want to be!

Young Queen, Young Queen

You must always believe in and
love yourself, even when no one else does.

Young Queen, Young Queen

Life will get tough at times,
but don't give up, and don't be afraid
to ask for help.

You are loved, appreciated, important, and needed in this world.

Never be afraid to speak your mind.
Your voice matters.

The world will pull you in different directions.

Trust yourself!

You know what's right and wrong.

People might lie, and even do the unexpected. Don't allow that to change who you are.

Everyone you like and everyone who likes you
may not be for you.

Young Queen, Young Queen

Never lower your values just to have company.
You are just fine as you are!

People's actions will show if they see your worth. If they don't, let them go.

Disrespect is a no, no. Don't accept negativity or allow anyone to disrespect you.

If you make a mistake, meaningfully apologize. If someone hurts you and apologizes, it's ok to accept the apology, and it's also ok to let that person go.

Your value goes far beyond your outer beauty. Your character, work ethic, and caring treatment of others is what truly matters! Don't ever let anything or anyone make you forget that.

Young Queen, Young Queen

Carry yourself well in all settings.

Young Queen, Young Queen

Loss, heartbreak, discouragement, anger, and down seasons will occur. Stand strong and continue to work through it all. The hardest times tend to produce the most glory.

Young Queen, Young Queen

Your actions and reactions will define you,
not your intentions or thoughts.
So make them count!

Work on you, love you, have personal projects, don't overextend yourself and realize it's ok to be selfish at times.

Use your creativity, your passion, and your will to create your future. Just because it hasn't happened before, doesn't mean that you can't make it happen.

Young Queen, Young Queen

Work on all of your dreams, push through life's many obstacles. Set goals, accomplish them, and then repeat! Never dim your lights for anyone.

There are other Queens available to help you. Actively search for an open, honest, and wise Queen to help groom you into the Queen that you would like to become.

Young Queen, Young Queen

Other Young Queens are your sisters; help them and allow them to help you as well. Everyone isn't an enemy, an envious person, or a gossip.

You are more than enough!

Trust God, talk to him, and include him in ALL of your plans.

You got it, go get it. Peace!

I Am Mr. Mentor, Peace

Author Bio

Justin Sims was born and raised in Mobile, Alabama. He received his Master's and Undergraduate degree from the University of Alabama at Birmingham. During his undergraduate career, Justin studied History and Secondary Education, while receiving his Master's in Information Engineering Management. This book was written by Justin Sims (IAMMRMENTOR) to awaken and push the inner Queen in all young women.

Growing up in a broken home, Justin was able to participate in mentoring programs via nonprofits and eventually able to return the favor by Directing the program (Team Focus) that greatly sewed into him as a child. After the program's grant ended, Justin was able to change careers, but still felt the urge to mentor young men. Knowing his true passion, Justin created a new platform and blog space for himself, **www.iammrmentor.co** on the websites, readers can read positive stories of black males, and contact Justin, (Mr. Mentor) directly.